Are you Highly Sensitive?

Discover all the keys

Manuela Pérez Chacón

Antonio Chacón

Juan Moisés de la Serna

Translated by Nicoleta Nagy

Tektime Editorial

2021

"Are you Highly Sensitive? Discover all the keys"

Written by Manuela Pérez Chacón, Antonio Chacón and Juan Moisés de la Serna

Translated by Nicoleta Nagy

1st Edition: August 2021

Juan Moisés de la Serna, 2021

© Tektime Editions, 2021

All rights reserved

Distributed by Tektime

https://www.traduzionelibri.it

The total or partial reproduction of this book is not allowed, nor its incorporation into a computer system, nor its transmission in any form or by any means, electronic, mechanical, by photocopy, by recording or other methods, without prior written permission from the editor.

The violation of the aforementioned rights may constitute an offence against intellectual property

Please contact Spanish Reproduction Rights Centre if you need to photocopy or scan any fragment of this work.

You can contact them at the www.conlicencia.com or by phone at 91 702 19 70/93 272 04 47.

About the authors:

Manuela Pérez Chacón

Manuela Pérez Chacón, Degree in Psychology, PhD Interuniversity Program in Human Resources Psychology University of Seville, and University of Valencia. Specialist in Clinical Psychology. Specialist in Industrial Psychology. University Specialist in Special Education: Therapeutic Pedagogy. Professional expert in psychological disorders in children and adolescents. Master's Degree in Occupational Risk Prevention, Safety, Hygiene, Ergonomics and Psychosociology.

Psychology professional with more than 10 years of experience in the area of health and prevention of psychosocial risks. Specialized in clinical therapeutic intervention and work psychology. Expert in Children and Youth Psychological Disorders. Founding member of the Infant-Juvenile Mental Health Unit of Puerta del Sur Hospital (USMIJ - Jerez Clinic). Gold Medal for Professional Merit awarded by the General Council of Industrial Relations and Labour Sciences, PREVER Awards 2018, for her research in the field of Psychosocial Risks in Organizations. Collegiate member of the Official College of Psychologists of Western Andalusia number AN-

06014.

President of the Spanish Association of High Sensitivity Professionals (HSP Spain). Psychologist specialized in HSP (highly sensitive people) and referenced in Spain as an expert in High Sensitivity. Disseminator and lecturer specialized in Child Psychology and Sensory Processing Sensitivity in children. First Spanish person certified as a specialized psychologist in High Sensitivity. (Acknowledged Professional by Elaine Aron). She has had interviews with well-known media such as Cadena SER, La1 of RTVE and El País.

Antonio Chacón

Expert in psychosocial risks with 15 years of experience in Third Party Prevention Services (SPA). PhD in Human Resources Psychology (University of Seville). Assistant Professor in the Master's Degree Program for Occupational Risk Prevention and in the Master's Degree Program for Integrated Systems (Universidad International de La Rioja – UNIR).

Founder of the Association of Psychologists and Professionals of High Sensitivity (PAS Spain). Awarded with the Cross of Honor by Safety and Health at Work and with the Gold Medal by the Europe Forum for Professional

Prestige. Disseminator of the Trait of High Sensitivity in Organizations.

Juan Moisés de la Serna

PhD in Psychology and Master's Degree in Neuroscience and Behavioral Biology. University professor.

Now his research focuses on the potential factors influencing with COVID-19 and on the short and long term psychological and neurological complications after being infected with SARS-CoV-2, in humans.

According to researchgate.net the most widely read author in Spain in 2020.

Scientific disseminator with more than thirty published books on Psychology and Neuroscience topics including AD; PS; ASD; ADHD; EQ; MSD; HIQ.

PROLOGUE

If you suspect that you may be a highly sensitive person, these pages will clear your doubts. This book is meant to be informative and support those of us who work "helping" others, as well as a call to parents, bosses or educators who interact with highly sensitive people.

First of all, we need to clarify that we all are sensitive, to a greater or lesser degree, but there is also a percentage of people who are highly sensitive, a factor that needs to be taken into consideration when educating, dealing with others, and living together.

The book is intended to make it easier for you to identify whether you possess the trait of high sensitivity, it is also essential to identify this trait in others since you could be a mother, father or brother of a highly sensitive person, or husband, teacher, or co-worker.

Contents

Chapter 1 Introduction to High Sensitivity

With these pages the authors hope that you will be able to identify the traits of high sensitivity as well as the psychological consequences. In this book you will find valuable experiences, studies, and scientific bases.

The experiences of highly sensitive people are without a doubt very useful examples to increase awareness among those interested in high sensitivity, for the importance of going to professionals specialized in this subject, whether psychologists, counsellors, pediatricians, and psychiatrists trained in High Sensitivity who will be able to offer solutions to the problems that may arise.

The reader should keep in mind that being highly sensitive is not similar to having a disorder, although it may be accompanied by certain difficulties which must be addressed properly.

Becoming aware of the existence of the High Sensitivity Trait among the people around us is as important as knowing who to turn to when we want or need solutions.

1.1. Defining High Sensitivity.

While the highly sensitive person is currently considered to possess an underlying innate trait, based on several characteristics that encompass a special cognitive ability to process information, awareness of subtle stimuli, emotional reactivity and easily over-stimulated, this concept has changed over time.

It should be noted that it has not been until the emergence of psychology as a science in which knowledge about the cognitive characteristics of the person begins to be studied and systematized.

Once knowledge evolved it began to be concerned with the particular cases not present throughout the entire population, while knowledge about psychopathology evolved and it was effectively intervened.

One of the best-known advances was the emergence of the concept of IQ, a measure of the ability to resolve a series of tests, designed and prepared by psychologists, which follow strict control standards, established by psychometry so that the results are valid and reliable for the population to which they are applied.

It can predict the level of academic success, and thus also the professional future of the students, long before they are able to be aware of their skills; it is also used in staff selection, to find the ideal candidate for the position, who does not have to be the best qualified, nor the one with the most experience.

While the IQ has been equated to the very concept of intelligence, it has been questioned over time, understanding that it is not a unitary thing but that there are various intelligences such as spatial intelligence, verbal intelligence, mathematical intelligence, musical intelligence, ...

The evolution of the concept of intelligence has allowed to analyze different aspects of the human being that until then had not been contemplated such as the least or the greatest stimuli processing capacity.

Thus, during the first half of the twentieth century Dabrowski (1948) developed the Theory of Emotional Development to explain qualitatively different levels of human development, which he called *The Theory of Positive Disintegration.*

This theory tries to explain certain differentiating cognitive characteristics, such as hypersensitivity or the high level of concentration and abstraction demonstrated by certain people, establishing five levels: primary integration, one level disintegration, spontaneous multilevel disintegration, organized multilevel disintegration, and finally secondary integration.

The concept of over-cxcitability which refers to the

inherited trait continues to be used from this theory, therefor the greater the over-excitability the greater the capacity and the power of development.

The author indicates that over-excitability can be seen in five areas: psychomotor, emotional, intellectual, sensitive, and imaginative, that is to say, these are the areas where it could stand out.

1.2. The Profile of the Highly Sensitive Person

At the present moment, a lot of research supports the existence of a particular way of feeling, thinking and interacting, thus it has been estimated that High Sensitivity is present in approximately 20% of the population (Aron and Aron, 1997), the highly sensitive person being given the acronym HSP and highly sensitive children HSC, who have a peculiar way of processing information and are also very creative, but as a counterpoint can experience high levels of stress very easily so sometimes they avoid certain social activities.

Among the characteristics of these people, it is found that they are good observers, they look even at the most subtle details, they also feel more bothered than the rest in the face of high levels of stimulation, such as noise and crowds, showing strong emotional responses, in addition approximately 70% are introverted.

As for gender there are as many sensitive men as there are women (Aron,1996), and although the presence of testosterone can have some later effect, the culture in which they live is the one that will make a difference in their sensitivity, since in some cultures men are forced to hide their sensitivity to look more like a typical man and avoid social problems.

While high sensitivity has so far been talked about as if it were a unique feature, some research has suggested that within this group it is possible to distinguish three groups of environmental sensitivity evidenced by the highly sensitive child scale and identification of sensitivity groups, published in Developmental Psychology (Pluess, 2017).

This instrument distinguishes the highly sensitive population, approximately 25 to 35%, from those with an intermediate sensitivity, between 41 and 47%; and those with low sensitivity between 20 and 35%.

It should be noted that there are many qualities that are visible and latent in a highly sensitive person, for example, they possess artistic talent linked to the creativity they manifest. Professionals or amateurs, the HSP demonstrate passion for some kind of art, whether musical, architectural, pictorial, etc., so it is common that they express themselves with phrases such as, "I could not live without my paintings" or "I am deeply in love with jazz since I was very young".

Their social relationships can also be fruitful if they want, since highly sensitive people are more aware of the thoughts and emotions of others, thus obtaining more information from the nonverbal language of the other person and become more intuitive, being able to guess what the other thinks or feels at a given time. This gives them the virtue of understanding the other person or knowing if they are lying for example, this is evidenced by phrases like "I fully understand how my child feels" or "What happened hurts me as much as it hurts them".

Any personal relationship can be very fruitful for a HSP since they are thoughtful and act more attentively and conscientiously, evaluating future causes and consequences and they not only care about others and society, but they also care about the environment. The mind of a HSP analyzes the process of how things came to be how they are, what will happen depending on the action, so they have reflections like, "what will happen if I do not approve everything in June" or "what would happen if everyone had electric cars".

HSP are usually considerate people, due to their great empathy, because they learn naturally to understand how the other feels and develop a considerate and sometimes suggestive way of addressing others, being able to express themselves with phrases such as, "Is it okay if we do so?" or "I suggest everyone give their opinion".

Other qualities of highly sensitive people are the harmony with nature, animals, the beach, or plants. Highly sensitive people discover that nature has an effect on them that transmits them calm and relaxation.

The High Sensitivity or Sensitivity of Sensory Processing is expressed as an awareness of the subtleties of stimuli, and the excess of stimuli manifests in their behaviour. This extreme sensitivity can be associated with perfectionism, the intense and excessive way to generate ideas and vulnerability to noises, smells, or textures. We can relate it to creativity, the ability to understand others and feel what others feel, the sense of justice, and respect for the other person.

Dabrowski observed how creative people showed higher levels of empathy, moral responsibility, self-reflection, and sensitivity. During times of crisis, they show symptoms related to internal conflict, feelings of inferiority, guilt, anxiety, or hopelessness.

Other more current research (Aron, Aron and Jagiellowicz, 2012) has shown that what we previously thought was introversion, shyness, empathy, hyperactivity, creativity, and other behavioural factors, when they come together in the same person and are shown to have been born with them, form a trait that has been called the Trait of the highly sensitive person. Although people born with this trait have a lot in common, each one also has their uniqueness and above all, each forms their personality depending on the life that they live.

The main characteristics of the highly sensitive person,

present from birth and lasting throughout the existence of the individual, affecting in turn all areas of their life are as follows (Aron, 2010):

1. Depth of cognitive processing. It is the most peculiar trait of the HSP, although it cannot be directly observed it is inferred from their behavior, and inferred from their thinking.

An indicator of this appears as a deep and intense reflection on each new situation in the subject's life, collecting a lot of information from around them and thinking about it deeply before acting, which leads them to arduous decision-making and requires more reaction time for each task.

This reflection leads to a stronger emotional reaction, where everything else affects them, they also manage to generate unusual and creative ideas due to this passionate and underlying way of processing information. They can also show a surprising degree of knowledge about themselves or others, a sense of long-term consequences and a great capacity for cognitive interpretation in the face of conversations or tasks.

2. Over-stimulation. For the HSP the high level of stimulation leads them to high levels of arousal, so at the environmental level, they feel more stressed by noise, chaotic situations, meeting deadlines, etc.

Regarding social stimulation, they feel more emotionally affected by perceiving more the details of the environment, which manifests itself by showing unusual nervousness, ongoing complaints, or problems with changes.

In cases where very high levels of arousal occur, this will be reflected in an increase in the activation of the sympathetic nervous system, generating a fight-flight response and thus causing discomfort and poor performance, since cognitive ability decreases generating confusion or affecting short-term memory, which can occur for example when doing tests, speaking in public, talking to strangers, playing sports, or are observed during a workout.

3. Emotional reactivity. Highly sensitive people have a greater ability to respond emotionally to every event in life, i.e., they feel more intensely positive and negative emotions, as well as being characterized by their inevitable feeling of empathy for others.

HSP are very sentimental people, who are excited about many things, and can present nostalgia of the past, feel compassion for the most disadvantaged, or cry more easily of joy, sadness or simply gratitude, they can also be more tending to be affectionate, to laughter, to subtle irony or to find in some kind of artistic creation the meaning of many things.

Emotional intensity as an indication of high sensitivity can be observed in exaggerated behaviours, in which the person appears to be at the end of the emotion generated, manifesting an eye-catching or "antisocial" lack of emotional regulation.

4. Sensory Sensitivity. Highly sensitive people notice subtle details that other people overlook, such as signs of nonverbal communication or small changes in a place, so sensory sensitivity arises from the processing of stimuli, not from the sense organs themselves, and such sensitivity is expressed in such a way that the individual is more impacted by the entry of sensory stimuli, such as annoying lights, intense odours, unforeseen noises, or rough textures.

In certain cases, it can also manifest itself as a low sensory threshold, with the ability to differentiate subtle sensations or with a low tolerance to the entry of sensory stimuli. It should be noted that when talking about perceived sensory stimuli, we mean both positive and negative. An individual may not tolerate the smell of a certain perfume, be able to distinguish the ingredients when trying a new food, or always wear sunglasses to protect themselves from the light they consider intense.

» Angela, 38-year-old employee

Angela had problems with the air conditioning temperature of the office, as well as difficulty setting boundaries assertively. She didn't want to be called picky like her siblings called her at home when they were little, but she also didn't know how to avoid it, so she visited numerous specialists until she ruled out that she might be hypersensitive to temperature.

Desperate in the face of the attitude of her peers, she spent summers with scarf, socks, and cardigan, to which it was concluded that she was unable to successfully regulate the cold in the workplace.

She also couldn't stand the smell of the environment and disguised it spraying air freshener several times during the workday, although her difficulty in saying "no" went far beyond the temperature problem, which is why she always worked longer hours to finish files that did not correspond to her.

She went out for coffee when she was invited, without her even liking coffee. She had no partner, no friends and her family were very distant, so she tried to keep all she had left, her job even though it was costing her her mental health.

Angela did not know how to manage her emotions,

which had led her to generate anxiety in the work context, and she also did not have adequate social skills, which had generated her fear of failure and interaction with others.

1.3. Is there a genetic component in high sensitivity?

One of the most controversial issues related to highly sensitive people has been in relation to its origin, that is, whether it is an inherited characteristic or it is the environment that allows some individuals to acquire and develop this sensitivity.

Although its origin has traditionally been attributed exclusively to a genetic basis excluding the environmental role, as raised by Francis Galton in the nineteenth century for the case of intelligence, who defended an Innatist theory, genetics is now considered to play an important role, but is not exclusive in the development of high sensitivity.

This has gone from defending a deterministic stance of genetics to giving it a leading role in development, i.e., now talking about genetic potential, thus favorable potential allows to achieve higher levels of sensitivity while limited genetic potential hinders the development of sensitivity.

But while we talk about the genetics of high sensitivity we have to mention the important role of the family, that is, the "cradle" will determine the possibilities of development, so if the family knows and learns how to manage the high sensitivity the child will be able to allow and help develop it, just as you would with talent for sports or music; however, if the family doesn't know or understand the child's characteristics, it's hard to make it easier to develop it.

From a young age, HSC benefit from being well-reared. Good environments during childhood generate optimal support to absorb both the information and the values they are intended to instill. It also leads to better management of emotions and stimuli in adulthood. For example, highly sensitive patients with panic disorder improve compared to people that are not HSP, due to the ease of understanding the role of over stimulation in their symptoms.

The family is first social environment in which the child forms emotional bonds of special transcendence for proper and optimal development. Childhood therefore has a human aspect and a social aspect, being fundamental in their growth the attitude that the adult maintains toward the child, thus the quality of adult child interaction and the bonds that flourish in the family will mark the psychological, social, and emotional evolution of the child.

Parents and educators should keep in mind that the variation in the behaviour of a highly sensitive child has an unalterable basis due to the genetic component of their trait, first social context, so it is essential to attend to the individual development of each child, considering their needs.

Diaz and Diaz-Sibaja (2005), tell us that normal behaviour in children depends on factors such as age, personality, and development of the child, as well they offer parenting guidelines or educational styles to the pattern of complex behaviour that includes specific behaviours to achieve changes in children, that is, they are not considered parenting guidelines to the deviant behaviours of negligent parents.

Parenting patterns are therefore behaviours based on controlling and socializing, aimed at achieving the emotional and behavioural adaptation of the child in society. Choosing one educational style over another should depend on the characteristics of the child and their response to the style that is being implemented.

MacCoby and Martin (1983) establish a categorization of parenting styles based on a typology of four educational styles: Democratic, Permissive, Authoritarian, and Indifferent.

Regarding highly sensitive children, we know that they are overexcited and over-stimulated more easily than other children and require more peace of mind around them, as well as rest times to process their experiences, so it would be best for them to be educated by graduating sensitivity and affection, responding according to the child's demand.

A managerial, authoritarian, or demanding educational style does not consider the emotional aspect of parent-child relationships important. These parents turn to obedience, to authority, for the child to comply with the standards, set clear and explicit rules, sometimes developing the use of power to set the course.

Such educated children have gaps in social skills, low self-esteem and even depression, and if they are highly sensitive children, as we know they are largely aware of the norms by their nature and need nothing more than a gentle reminder.

It is therefore advisable to remember the rules privately, which will encourage them to comply and avoid the need to resort to hard discipline toward them, trying not to highlight what is expected that the child achieves, since it is enough to praise their efforts.

It is also important that parents avoid comparing them to other children or siblings, because HSC are quite self-critical so they try to follow the rules and if they are told that they made a mistake they will think about it in depth, thus causing harmful ruminative thinking and if also punished their self-esteem will be damaged.

Keep in mind that it is only needed a change in the tone of voice, or a firm look sometimes, so that the child realizes their wrong attitude and tries to improve it.

A permissive, complacent, or compassionate style does not require responsible or mature behaviour in children, allowing children to impose their own criteria and for parents to justify behaviours in their children aimed at deviating from established social norms.

Children educated in permissive families have higher self-esteem, but also a greater tendency to get involved in problems, so in the case of highly sensitive children, they tend to feel guilty if they get involved in problems developing guilt as a learning strategy, so as a parent you should not fail to correct the behaviour of your HSC, since what generates greater culpability is precisely the total lack of discipline.

An unreliable, insensitive, or indifferent style implies unreliable parenthood, parents who do not get emotionally involved and try to make their children's education as effortless.

Children living in this parental style end their upbringing with deficits in sociability and high emotional dependence. This style is totally contradictory to achieve a good upbringing of a highly sensitive child, which demands communication and empathy during their growth.

Keep in mind that it's important to alert your HSC to changes in routines, trips, or events, so they can adapt, improve communication, and avoid problems, equally empathizing with them will prevent when they're over-excited that some HSC retract and look shy, or unmotivated, or that they are crying and irritable, or seem hyperactive or even aggressive.

To try to control the behaviour of a HSC child in these situations, you have to help them find the cause that has led them to feel like this, and later explain with a story or anecdote what they can do next time they feel like this.

A democratic style combines an attitude of demanding parents but affectionate at once, where they see their children as active participants in the educational process and attach great importance to the affection and emotions of the child.

These parents observe their children's behaviour and impose clear criteria while establishing a priority order regarding compliance with standards and promoting dialogue to reason.

The methods used are based more on positive reinforcement than punishment achieving that children value themselves more and acquire good social skills.

This educational style, ideal for any child, is especially recommended for raising highly sensitive children which being a minority should not be subject to judgement or criticism.

This type of parenting style can help them establish close ties of friendship in their relationships with other children, because you have to keep in mind that the HSC are good at making friends, but at their own pace, and if possible one by one; It is also advisable instilling enthusiasm for some artistic area, social assistance or nature and animals while promoting relations with the environment.

But although so far we have focused on the family, in the middle of the twentieth century is given greater weight to the role of education and thus the influence of the environment, being made a clear distinction between the concept of neuronal maturation development and on the other learning. The former has an important genetic base, while the second is largely determined by the conditions of the environment based on this theory arises the intellectual environment, which defends that development in this intellectual case but it is equally applicable to the sensitivity, requires certain environmental conditions such as an intellectually rich atmosphere, adequate supply and an emotional climate warm and mediator; the absence of these conditions will hinder the development of the child's potential.

Regarding the influence of the school is noted that some highly sensitive children can be defined as non-imposing wise leaders, although initially they may seem timid, due to their style of information processing, when they get a friendly environment and where members feel important, become best friends and those with better initiatives and ideas.

Door's (2018) points out that there is a difference between unity and uniformity, and schools should foster unity, because that is the wealth of people, in their differences, while uniformity instead focuses only on equality or following the same pattern.

Accepting the existence of individual differences and encouraging those differences starting in schools is a must.

While so far, the educational plans have included numerous programs and projects to improve pupils with special educational needs, more and more schools accept and encourage these differences with respect and education in values, so we need to facilitate learning. It is our responsibility as parents and educators.

Laws cover educational attention to diversity, ensure equity in education and development for everyone with personalized attention depending on the needs of each student. The LOE and LOMCE, have opted for an educational reform involving: "A set of measures to improve the conditions so that all students can acquire and express their talents and achieve their full personal and professional development, and support equal opportunities".

Both the highly sensitive pupils and students with high capacities have something in common. Both have a special educational need and share a kind of intelligence which we call "sensitive intelligence" and have the need to feel every situation, experience the thrill of every circumstance and connect with what's around them, looking to do it naturally without pretending to be accepted.

References

Aron, A., Ketay, S., Hedden, T., Aron, IN, Rose Markus, H. and Gabrieli, J.D. (2010). Temperament trait of sensory processing sensitivity moderates cultural differences in neural response. Social Cognitive and Affective Neuroscience, 5 (2-3), 219-226.

Aron, E. N. and Aron, A. (1997). Sensory-processing sensitivity and its relation to introversion and emotionality. Journal of Personality and Social Psychology, 73(2), 345–368.

Aron, E. N., Aron, A., and Jagiellowicz, J. (2012). Sensory Processing Sensitivity: A Review in the Light of the Evolution of Biological Responsivity. Personality and Social Psychology Review, 16 (3), 262-282. https://doi.org/10.1177/1088868311434213

Dabrowski, K. (1964). Positive Disintegration. Little Brown.

Dabrowski, K. (1967). Personality-shaping through positive disintegration. Little Brown.

Dabrowski, K. (1972). Psychoneurosis is not an illness. Gryf Publications.

Dabrowski, K., Kawczak, A. and Piechowski, M. M. (1970). Mental growth: through positive disintegration. Gryf Publications.

Dabrowski, K. and Piechowski, M. M. (1977). Theory of levels of emotional development. Vol. I and II. Dabor Science Publications.

Diaz-Garcia M. I. and Diaz-Sibaja, M. A. (2005). Everyday problems of child behavior in M. I. Comeche, and M.A. Vallejo (Coor.), Handbook of behavioral therapy in childhood. Dykinson.

Pluess, M., Assary, E., Lionetti, F., Lester, K. J., Krapohl, E., Aron, E. N., and Aron, A. (2018). Environmental Sensitivity in Children: Development of the Highly Sensitive Child Scale and Identification of Sensitivity Groups. Developmental Psychology, 54 (1), 51-70. https://doi.org/10.1037/dev0000406

Chapter 2. Identifying High Sensitivity

Although high sensitivity is a relatively recent concept and currently there isn't sufficient evidence to be recognized and adequately addressed this does not mean that there are no contentious or unresolved issues as discussed in this chapter, but what is undeniable is the existence of a part of the population that has been "suffering" the lack of understanding of their peculiarities by others.

So unlike what happens with some students such as with the case of high ability or ADHD, which are regulated as pupils with special educational needs, which go through a psycho educational assessment, and whose reports extract specific actions for each child depending on their characteristics, in the case of the HSC their needs are not yet recognized, not even evaluated to know what they need nor there are protocols for intervention in the classroom, i.e., there is still much progress to be made on the part of society awareness about the need to recognize the peculiarities of HSC students.

2.1. Differences and similarities between High Sensitivity and High Capacity

It is important to clarify that developmental and social differences may exist during the growth of any child, i.e., each child has a rhythm in their development, and some reach some skills before others, which does not mean better or worse in that skill. In addition, each has three types simultaneously: age, mental age, chronological and emotional, and if that was not enough, we must bear in mind that these ages do not always evolve or grow at the same pace in the same child.

Specifically, for gifted children often there are differences between their mental age and actual or chronological age, while at other times the difference is between their emotional age and mental age, i.e., there is often no correlation between their age and other important development aspects presenting an intellectual, social, and emotional difference from children of the same age.

Children with high capacities are born researchers who need to create, imagine, showing differences from other children in games and motivation, being active and also in the way they speak.

Some clues to take into consideration to determine if a child is gifted intellectually is their high performance in some subjects, as well as having a more advanced language that other children of the same age. They could be asking questions that surprise adults, possessing a peculiar logical reasoning and a unique way of learning.

In addition to all this and to identify them, we can look at the things they usually do, what are fun things for them and their behaviour when they play or relate in a group.

Identifying children with high abilities is a difficult task that requires time and evaluation should be done by professionals. Due to the fact that they only use IQ, it is incomplete to diagnose students with more talent, so the high intellectual quotient is one more thing to consider, however, other factors should be evaluated, such as sensitivity, creativity, academic skills, leadership, socio-emotional characteristics, or artistic area.

Piechowski (1979) considers that traditionally the emphasis was on intellectual and other types of skills, leaving little room for imagination and feelings, defining the high intellectual ability as that multidimensional phenomenon that interrelates the specific talent, how favorable is the environment and unique personality characteristics.

Although the most common so far has been the identification of high capacity through intelligence questionnaires, highly sensitive people are characterized by a rich and intense inner life and creativity and emotional intensity because of their great subjective experience, generate matches between HSC and people with high capacities.

We must clarify that this is not a matter of degree, but the difference is qualitative. Both types of people live more complex, brash, and penetrating experiences.

Silverman (2018) tells of people with high capacities stating that "Giftedness is an accelerated development, but in adulthood this advantage becomes a moral value, moral sensitivity, creativity, empathy, the willingness to help others". Besides this author believes that for every gifted child recognized by their family and at school there is another gifted child that is not recognized anywhere.

This is a recurring problem where there are often few evaluation protocols to detect HSP, to which we must add that sometimes wrong diagnoses make parents believe that their children have high capacities when they are highly sensitive.

To this must be added that individual differences are not always accepted, and sometimes the school or the family encourage each child to reaches a certain pattern, say, for example are excluded those who do not play football or do not get good grades or are not very communicative, as a result, many highly sensitive people, as well as those with high capacities try to fit the mold, putting on the costume every day to look or appear to be, the person others expect.

2.2. The brain development in the High Sensitivity

One of the characteristics of highly sensitive people is based on the form of certain perceived environmental stimuli, especially those pertaining to perception through the senses, and the skin may be one of the sensitive points, as well as the hearing or the sight.

While many people do not care if there is too much light, if it's too hot or conversely too cold, are not even aware of the high volume on television, or, they are indifferent to what they eat, highly sensitive people are affected and are often startled by noise, can easily perceive a new ingredient in the food, even complain when they feel excessive heat or cold or believe that there is too much light in the room, even if it is a subjective perception.

We could say that they require a time incorporated into their routine, allowing a space to breathe silence and tranquillity, requiring, for example, more time to relax after a busy day, all of which means a different neural processing from the rest of the population.

With regard to neural findings high sensitivity differences were found which leads them to be more sensitive to stimulation, such as hearing, responding more strongly to sound, both in amplitude and duration, hypersensitivity has also been seen in the other senses, either in vision, touch, taste, or smell.

Other research supports the depth of cognitive processing, considered the most important corner of the trait of high sensitivity and also the most difficult to observe with the naked eye.

A comparative study of brain activity of highly sensitive people and non highly sensitive people (Jagiellowicz, 2011) was published in the journal Social Cognitive and Affective Neuroscience.

The participants had to find the differences between two very similar in contrast with two explicitly different images. As a result, it was found that highly sensitive people showed greater activity in brain areas responsible for perceptual complexity and detection of details, i.e., the highly sensitive participants used more parts of the brain involved in deep processing and elaborate information.

A year earlier in the same journal he had published a study comparing the relationship between non highly sensitive people and highly sensitive people, born, and educated in two completely contrasting cultures, individualistic (USA) and collectivist (Asia).

The aim of the study was to observe the brain activity while subjects performed perceptual tasks varying in difficulty. The result of which was that the brain activity of those who were not highly sensitive, requiring extra effort when the task was more difficult for people of their culture, in contrast to the brains of highly sensitive subjects, there was no difference regarding the effort in both tasks. The authors of the study concluded that the perceptive capacity of highly sensitive people delved beyond the limits of their cultural bias.

Meanwhile an investigation using fMRI on brain characteristics of people with high sensitivity (Acevedo, 2014), was published in the scientific journal Brain and Behaviour.

The subjects in the study, observed photographs of loved ones and others of strangers, both showing on their faces positive, negative, and neutral emotions.

The research findings reported that highly sensitive people, had high activity of mirror neurons, the anterior insular region and the ventral tegmental area, areas of the brain associated with empathy and motivation.

This study indicates that highly sensitive people are more able to receive external stimuli that relate to emotions as well, the study showed that during the process, highly sensitive people, were better able to recognize the surrounding reality and relate with their work.

A special mention in terms of the emotional brain where it has been observed how often they have greater connectivity between the anterior cingulate cortex and frontal cortex, which explain the satisfaction of curiosity about things. It also explains a differential emotional processing showing a hypersensitivity to emotions, including at the suffering of symptoms associated with depression or anxiety.

But these are not the only brain changes found, and thanks to neuroplasticity each individual can "shape" their brain differently than the rest, despite similar experiences offered by a shared culture means that there are great similarities among individuals.

» Leo, 40 years old retired

Leo had symptoms of depression and lived alone. Throughout his life he had piggybacked what he called his "backpack full of difficulties." Had been divorced for one year, had a daughter for whom he had been attending court hearings for food and visitation. Before this he suffered an accident in which he fell from the balcony of his house which left him with some physical consequences and took him to an early retirement. His economic situation was good because he had a public position from a young age and that would pay him his entire life.

Years ago, he "fooled around" with drugs and alcohol,

something that he controlled since he became a father, but acknowledged that it marked his adolescence. His childhood was sad, he always felt the "ugly duckling" of his eight siblings, he was the smallest. His earliest memories as a child, loom very elderly parents who could barely fend for themselves, and his older brothers put in a residence, leaving the small, including Leo. He had always felt misunderstood by his family, he never had good friends and on top a relationship without a happy ending.

2.3. Emotional processing in High Sensitivity

In regard to their emotions, highly sensitive people are characterized by their desire to cry more easily and for certain reasons for which a person non-HSP would not cry, but also feel happier in situations that make them feel good, that is, emotions tend to move to the ends of a continuum.

As we know emotions are very difficult to control and are one of the vertices of the triangle formed by thoughts, actions, and emotions, can not change on their own and rely on the other two vertices for tiny changes.

To understand the human mind, sometimes we use synonymously feelings and emotions, however, we can explain each of the terms separately.

Emotions, we know occur in a part of the brain called

the limbic system, are the set of neurochemical and hormonal responses which make us react in a certain way to a particular stimulus, whether it is an external stimulus such as seeing a painting, or an internal stimulus, such as remembering a loved one at a particular time.

We could say that because our limbic system acts in an almost predetermined way, since the brain not only stores data but learns to react moved by emotions that cause the experiences, we associate experiences with emotions, we feel good remembering nice places and, we feel bad knowing that we need a surgical intervention, and to the contrary, having travelled to beautiful places makes us want to travel more, having been under the knife we do not want to return to an operation unless it is necessary, or there is either interesting reason.

This is what a feeling does, evaluate or give value to an experience, that is, the feeling is a conscious experience that includes reflection and thought, while emotion is basic and primitive, but we can't isolate a feeling from the emotion that appears, since feelings and emotions go together, which is why the distinction is more theoretical than practical.

Paul Ekman (1934), American psychologist who pioneered the study of emotions, said there are six basic emotions: sadness, happiness, surprise, disgust, fear, anger. We can also name other very common basic emotions such as feeling threatened and irritation.

Remember that in the development of highly sensitive people both genetic and environmental aspects influence, which in turn will affect the intensity of emotions and depth in processing information.

Vygotsky, in deepening the decisive influence of the environment on the cognitive development in children, observed that our behaviour tends to keep our body in balance with the environment. The more complex the interaction between the organism and the environment, the more winding becomes the balancing process and consequently the process to facilitate the balance is not possible without always appearing some complications, there will be some imbalance in favour of the environment or of the organism.

Thus, all sensitive people react more deeply to those situations or behaviours that have generated them a thrill, knowing that promotes emotion or promotes cognitive processing, so what is processed longer has an emotional component, therefore the more processing the more excitement and so on.

A greater intensity of emotion, more vulnerable to feelings of fear, anxiety, or sadness, which often result in anxiety disorders, depression, or phobias, considering that the stress is in the person, not in the situation, so the same situation or certain behaviours, can bother and even cause pathological symptoms to a highly sensitive person.

High levels of emotion can become a negative influence that awakens in the person, reflected in the emotional state of extreme levels of emotion such as anger, guilt, fear, and nervousness.

It is well known that high levels of emotions in a person, the result of symptoms of a disorder, end up defining their personality as neurotic, but neuroticism is not synonymous with high sensitivity in all its sense.

Both anger and guilt or nervousness in highly sensitive people are the result of unfortunate experiences at an early age and are not due to the trait itself so highly sensitive people with troublesome childhoods, are more likely to feel negative affection compared to people who are not highly sensitive and have presented the same level of difficulty in their infancy.

Children's environment makes shyness present in sensitive people who had a difficult childhood, whose experiences gave rise to high levels of negative affect, though not all negative childhoods of sensitive people lead to the negative affect, highly sensitive people are also more likely to feel positive emotions more deeply.

Highly sensitive people whose childhoods have not

been traumatic and those who have leaned to manage their emotions, have a high probability of developing a low negative affect in certain situations, i.e., a state of calm and serenity, hence the importance of screening the trait early in children who begin to show problems because generally the earlier a defect is treated, the more effective the result.

It should be noted that we can not separate the intellectual from the emotional, since the need to learn and curiosity are also emotional needs, as are the emotions that motivate the person, and emotions move the latent intellect in people with more talent.

Dabrowski (1972) emphasized the role of emotions in human development with his theory of emotional development explaining that the interaction of the individual with the environment produces the Development Potential of the individual, consisting of talent, intelligence and over excitability, with inclination toward self growth.

The five over excitabilities of which Dabrowski speaks are: psychomotor, sensory, intellectual, imaginative, and emotional, underscoring the author's characteristic forms of expression, and indicating the development potential and therefore the high capacity of the person who possesses them.

These are people likely to experience positive

disintegration, this term is somewhat paradoxical, since at level 1 the individual believes that he is the centre of everything, making materialistic decisions, interested in money, power, consumerism, etc. and they no longer want to grow now that they have no inner questioning, always blame the other, get what they intend with their charms, but once achieved the goal, are not interested in the other person, in contrast, people of level 5 are able to control their instincts and their material needs and are in the pursuit of good for humanity.

References

Acevedo, B. P., Aron, E. N., Aron, A., Sangster, M. D., Collins, N., and Brown, L. L. (2014). The highly sensitive brain: an fMRI study of sensory processing sensitivity and response to others' emotions. Brain and Behavior, 4 (4), 580-594. https://doi.org/10.1002/brb3.242

Chavez-Eakle, R.A. (2008). Measuring overexcitability: Replication across five countries in Mendaglio S. (Ed.), Dabrowski's theory of positive disintegration (pp. 183- 199). Great Potential Press, Inc.

Ekman, P. (2007). Emotions revealed (2nd ed.). Henry Holt.

Maccoby, E. E. (1983). Social-emotional development and response to stressors in N. Garmezy and M. Rutter (Eds.) & Ctr for Advanced Study in the Behavioral Sciences, Inc, Stress, coping, and development in children (p. 217-234). Johns Hopkins University Press.

Piechowski, M. M. (1979). Developmental potential in N. Colangelo and R. T. Zaffrann (Eds), New Voices in counseling the gifted (pp. 25-57). Kendall Hunt Publishing.

Piechowski, M. M. and Colangelo, N. (1984). Developmental potential of the gifted. Gifted Child Quarterly 28, 80-88.

Silverman, L. K. (1998). Personality and learning styles of gifted children in J. Van Tassel-Baska-(Ed.), Excellence in educating gifted and talented learners (3rd ed., Pp. 29-65). Love Publishing Company.

Silverman. L. K. (2002). Upside-down brilliant: the visual-spatial learner. DeLeon Publishing.

Silverman, L. K. (2018). Assessment of Giftedness inn S. I. Pfeiffer (Ed.), Handbook of Giftedness in Children: Psychoeducational Theory, Research, and Best Practices (pp. 183-207). Springer International Publishing. https://doi.org/10.1007/978-3-319-10208-5_2

Vygotsky, L. S. (1972). The Psychology of Art. Journal of Aesthetics and Art Criticism, 30 (4), 564-566.

Chapter 3. How to be Highly Sensitive and not die trying

Differential psychology teaches us that each person reacts in their own way in the world and in their interaction with others, because the uniqueness of individuals is one of the basic facts of life.

Individual peculiarities appear immediately after birth and are surprisingly strengthened with progressive maturation. So, it can be said that no human being is equal to another, although there are certain similarities between people. These differences are reflected in certain characteristics, without the particular combination being identical, and are explained by a saying: "The product of diversity it is no longer the same."

Some people think their way of being is because they were born a certain way and can not change, however others believe life has led them to be as they are, and even blame others who feel have influenced them to be the way they are. But in reality, both types of people have a point, people are born and made, as the philosopher Ortega and Gasset had said it: "I am me and my circumstances".

Personality is the identity of a person; it is the set of qualities that they have and differentiate them from others. The personality traits of each individual are patterns that recur persistently in the way they perceive situations as well as their thinking schemes and way of relating to others.

The context is responsible for shaping the personality and depending on such factors as lived experiences and motivation, each person tends to direct their behaviour in one direction or another.

Another element of personality is the temperament. Knowing that we are all born with an innate one, is the most instinctive trait of the person and the first to manifest, however the character has a learnt component, i.e., it appears as a result of the experiences lived, character is part of the temperament which is molded with social interaction, so it will depend on the context and has a great cultural component.

In psychology, personality is the result of the interaction between temperament and character. It is the sum of the biological basis of a person plus the environment influences in which the individual is immersed. In the case of highly sensitive people, they are born with characteristics that we call innate characteristics of the HSP, which represent a part of their temperament.

Interacting with the environment, the environmental context is defining the personality of the subject in question, i.e., organizing emotions, behaviour, and thoughts, in the same way that no one can totally disassociate from their temperament, HSP can't get rid of their trait, although in both cases it is possible to shape certain aspects regarding the character and indirectly the temperament.

Another feature we need to consider is the emotional stability of a person, which depends on one's ability to react to stressful situations, frustration tolerance, coping skills and expectations.

Maladaptive emotional responses vary along a continuum, so that at one end we can place the emotionally stable person, and at the opposite end, would be the person with severe instability or borderline personality disorder.

People able to manage their negative emotions result in favorable behaviours, however, those others whom we call unstable, which are driven by extreme emotions, result in harmful behaviours, i.e., their performance is impaired.

Highly sensitive people are born with a lack of regulation of their emotional level, leading them unconsciously to extremes. So, if we are dealing with negative emotions, we could talk of higher vulnerable at the negative end and in the same way we could talk about positive emotions increased vulnerability to the positive extreme and therefore a greater need to learn to manage these negative emotions.

That is why, stable people would have coping strategies to react adaptively, and these resources can be acquired both naturally in the family, school, or through therapy in some cases.

In conclusion, we must distinguish between two totally different concepts but interrelated or with common elements: the personality trait that every individual presents for the simple fact of being a person and living in a context, and on the other hand the innate trait of highly sensitive person.

Going back to personality, the classical theories of personality explain the differences between individuals regarding the diversity of personalities, and often are not intellectual or performance capabilities but more temperamental characteristics that generate a variety base. Each person is distinguished by their own temperament, and the diversity of each individual has to do with both their way of relating to the environment as well as their ability to adapt to changes and new situations.

Temperament is determined according to each nervous system and is related to the endocrine influence. Knowing that the hormones released by this system play a decisive role in regulating mood and emotions we have different types of personalities which we know depend on various factors.

Eysenck (1965) through individual questionnaires and objective tests, realized a classification of personality based on two dimensions, emotional stability, and introversion/extroversion, resulting in four temperaments, melancholy, phlegmatic, choleric, and sanguine.

Cattell (1973) in turn defines personality as a person's behaviour in a given situation, which is explained on the basis of a specification equation and the confrontation of the behaviour with the evident temperament of the individual.

In his Theory of Traits, he sought to identify basic features that define all people which he called the Big Five: openness to experience, conscientiousness, extroversion, agreeableness, and neuroticism.

Michael Pluess and colleagues conducted a study in 2017 of environmental awareness in children through the development of an instrument applied to children and adolescents, which identified three groups with different levels of environmental sensitivity.

The results indicated that approximately 25-35% of the sample had low environmental sensitivity, meanwhile 41-47% had a median one and 20-35% of the subjects subjected to environmental sensitivity research presented high environmental sensitivity.

Theories that defend the differential susceptibility,

based on the person-environment interaction go beyond all classical theories of temperament and personality emphasizing that highly sensitive people are not sensitive only to the adverse aspects of the context, but also benefit from positive environments. There are different types of reactivity in children, even in similar environments, determined by emotional, mental, and behavioral characteristics.

Highly sensitive children are more susceptible to parenting styles used by parents, whether positive or negative. The children that are more susceptible to the environment, change their levels of negative emotionality (anxiety, anger, fear, etc.) as they mature and interact socially, i.e., learn to regulate their negative emotions. So, we could say that to some extent being born with the trait of high sensitivity, could be an indicator of greater environmental sensitivity.

Remember that the Highly Sensitive concept is characterized by a characteristic with which one is born and accompanies the person throughout their life. In the case of innate characteristics of high sensitivity, can lead to adverse factors sometimes difficult to control. We explain some of the problems associated with being HSP:

1. Overstimulation. The HSP is easily overstimulated

and excited by less stimulation than other people. Overstimulation leads to increased saturation leading to poor performance in school activities for children or work routines for adults. Some of the situations in which we see it reflected are public speaking, assessments, quizzes, crowded places, timed tests, etc. The result in minors it's usually seen in the rejection of certain activities and avoidance of certain places.

2. Low self-esteem. Problems associated with the culture in which the highly sensitive person is. In the East children with the highly sensitive trait are popular among their peers, to the contrary of the Western culture like ours. This directly affects the self-esteem of the individual when adding the experiences of rejection or failure can lead to low self-esteem or emotional distress.

3. Sociability. Highly sensitive people have a characteristic based on their trait, which makes them prefer to keep on the side in new situations so that they can explore, observe, and reflect before acting. This behaviour may create a bad first impression of the person to strangers. Some comments that unsettle the listener can be: "I can not stand being cold" or "I have to cut off all my clothes labels before getting dressed."

4. Constant concern. The emotional reaction of HSP is higher than that of other people in the same situation.

They can cry more easily and worry excessively. Dramatic films, or Disney films can be an ordeal for HSP, always trying to avoid that an animal is mistreated or a child left orphan.

5. Manias. Highly sensitive people may become very attentive to the little subtleties or realize small changes in their environment. Which can be misinterpreted as a mania. Interpret comments of others ("Now you talk about yourself as a famous person") and interpreting nonverbal language of others ("You don't believe what I'm telling you"), or, commenting on any physical changes of a person or place ("You changed again the curtains of the living room"), can lead to a negative view of the HSP in question for being "weird" or "maniac".

6. Anguish. Apparently sudden changes can cause feelings of distress in HSP, requiring an adjustment period to give free rein to the trait of analysis and reflection. To adjust the accommodation to changes that their nature calls them to avoid risks can be challenging for HSP.

7. Self-criticism and perfectionism. The characteristic of highly sensitive person leads them to observe every detail and analyze possible outcomes before acting, as opposed to most other people who tend to decide faster. They are slower than non-sensitive people in making decisions because they are more aware of the risks and

benefits. The motto of a HSP type is usually "do it slow but do it right". The negative result of perfectionism is based on the slowness in decision-making, in social situations can generate an image of lacking ability or appear to be less intelligent.

8. Agitation. Until they know the cause and have a good self-esteem, HSP often complain about exciting places or, of those environments that seem to them unaesthetic. Some common phrases of the HSP are, "I can not stand fluorescent lights" or "I can not go to nightclubs, the loud music makes me very nervous".

9. Error in interpretation. HSP can generate erroneous schemes of thinking perceiving reality more frequent or intense as other people because they perceive more intensely and feel more intensely feelings generated by bad experiences, remembering them for a long time. One of these erroneous thought patterns that are repeated in them, is called the error of interpretation, which is the anticipation that things will go wrong, considering the prediction of the future unchangeable. The fact that they have been harmed by bad experiences in childhood and adolescence justifies the cause.

10. Physical sensitivity. The immune system of the HSP is more reactive. They also have more psychosomatic illnesses and manifest more startle responses. Some

children are easily startled at an unexpected noise, mothers are surprised when they observe it and compare it with usual responses of other children. They repeat phrases such as "what a scare" or "it will give me something." Adults visit frequently the family doctor when they do not have anything.

11. Selective abstraction. This is a wrong thought pattern consisting of only looking at one type of information, the negative one, putting it above other experiences. HSP have an unusual interest in social justice and the environment. Children manifest it in sentences like "the teacher was angry with my friend, and they had no fault" or "poor little bird that died in the street next to the school, did you see it?" Because they can not help but sympathize to what they consider social injustices. Most children react to the anger of their parents or their teachers naturally, the HSP can not help but feel overwhelmed by every similar and everyday situation.

3.1. Self-Esteem and High Sensitivity

The manifestation of feelings makes the person highly sensitive, more sensitive to subtle stimuli, however, we could say that besides reflecting before acting, observing carefully, being preoccupied to do everything right or unusual ideas and creativity, are as a whole the main defining characteristic of the HSP.

This set of actions and thoughts is called Depth of Cognitive Processing and is the largest of the four pillars that form the innate trait of the highly sensitive person, which first feels, then thinks and finally acts, taking all the necessary time for this process.

Another characteristic of the trait, the almost constant awareness of others, defines the highly sensitive person as emotionally reactive showing high empathy toward others since they are able to capture even the most subtle of the messages emitted by the nonverbal language of another person.

Among the explanations for this emotionality, Acevedo (2014) studied the mirror neurons of highly sensitive people, which are responsible for the existence of this high empathy in people, fostering their ability to perceive the emotions of others. When the mirror neuron system is activated, the person feels sad if their child cries or, is happy if someone around them is happy.

But also, highly sensitive people will be sensitive to their needs and intense desires. Maslow (1943), in his hierarchy of human needs, describes the need for appreciation as well as the appreciation one has for themselves, self esteem, and the respect and the esteem received from others, something that will be enhanced in highly sensitive people, where acceptance of the other will play a decisive role in self-esteem.

We could say that self-esteem is that which everyone thinks of themselves, the idea they have of themselves on how they see themselves doing things, their preferences and performance in their relationships with others and also about the demands.

Although it should be noted that self-esteem and knowing yourself are not the same, but are related, as satisfaction increases when one succeeds in putting into practice the knowledge they have of themselves. For example, if a student knows that they are a good student and manages to get good grades will raise their self-esteem, as well it will improve their self-esteem if they meet the requirements set by themselves. For example, if they value their school grades and get a ten.

Despite this we must consider that others also influence their self-esteem when praising those behaviours or skills that are important to them. For example, their self-esteem will raise if they think they are very good at basketball and also their family applauds each basket at a game.

Usually, we see in society how children with high self-esteem feel proud of their accomplishments, assume responsibilities with ease, tolerate frustration, show enthusiasm, and express what they think and what they feel easily. However, people with low self-esteem, avoid situations that cause them anxiety, do not value their qualities, feel that others do not value them, blame their problems on others, they are intolerant of frustration and feel powerless in difficulties.

One of the complaints that parents express about the behaviour of their children is the negativity that they manifest. That constant "NO" from some children can be caused by low self-esteem, so some parents see a continuous and persistent "no" above all, "I do not want to go to school", "I will not pass the exam," "It's not my fault" or "I do not know where the socks are".

We need to keep in mind that each child is unique and can show low self-esteem in different ways. Parents need to observe their behaviour carefully to detect if it is irrational because seeking solutions on time is critical so that the irrational behaviour doesn't become a habit and ends up being part of their personality.

It is important to add that highly sensitive children may be more vulnerable to low self-esteem by the mere fact of being a minority among our population. So, the messages they receive for achievements are lower in a society that values as success attitudes based on impulsivity or competitiveness. Also, the innate characteristic of the HSC is that their feelings are more intense, so their emotions go to the end of the continuum, both the good ones and the bad ones resulting in self-satisfaction being more difficult to achieve due to greater self-demand.

One way to ensure better self-esteem in HSC, would be to inculcate that the sense of power is a good thing for them, which will make them trust that they can achieve what they propose themselves. Although the HSC are already responsible by nature, this being an advantage when it comes to instructing them in anything, their high empathy for others, may interfere if the instruction is geared toward the sense of power, because by nature HSC avoid competitiveness and all power has a component of it.

Some guidelines to help highly sensitive children to improve their self-esteem can be:

• Teach them to distinguish between situations they can face because they arc their sole responsibility and which not. We need to consider that HSC are very concerned with social injustice and can put the rights of others above their own. It is important to teach them to establish limits and learn to say "no" when necessary, especially among equals.

• Give them the opportunity to take decisions by giving them the opportunity to choose when it comes to personal issues, such as choosing clothing, toys, books, etc. Above all we must allow them to do those things that show they are capable of doing, to foster the feeling of pride in their own abilities.

• Teach them to not blame others or fate for their failures by teaching them to manage their feelings. Self-control of their emotions will be an advantage in situations that can cause fear, anger, or anxiety.

• Teaching them social skills can help them learn to communicate with others successfully and avoid problems with peers. Younger ones can start by learning to take turns, not interrupt when adults talk or ask with, please.

3.2. Decision-making and High Sensitivity

20% of the population possesses the high sensitivity trait as current research indicates. Curiously the same percentage was found in animals, demonstrated in studies with fruit flies as well as primates (Suomi 1987, 1991). Biologists speak of two general strategies in animals, bold against withdrawn, eagle against pigeon, insensitive against sensitive.

In the first category presenting an impulsive or bold behaviour, their strategy is to move quickly and energetically to feeding and breeding opportunities, while the latter, who are the minority, tend to develop a survival approach based on risk avoidance observing the subtleties in a situation before acting. Both strategies, "act now" or "first observe and think" can be considered successful, depending on the conditions of the environment.

In humans, the most sensible strategy of scanning the environment and paying attention to detail, thinking, and feeling before and during a behaviour has been observed in functional magnetic resonance imaging. It is a strategy that allows greater qualms about the subtleties and can generate high levels of awareness and creativity. Although the downside of this strategy is that there is greater potential to be stimulated and anxious by stressful life events.

Gerstenberg (2012), compared HSP and non-HSP by performing complex perceptual tasks. Under a series of letters L in different positions there was a hidden T and rotated, which subjects of the experiment had to find. The result showed that highly sensitive people were faster and had more hits.

» Marcos, 17-years old student

Marcos was in high school. His grades were excellent in subjects that require memorization since he spent a lot of time on his schoolwork, however he found difficult subjects such as mathematics or physics, in which after many hours of study would only get a five. He had always been very responsible, hardworking, good friend of his friends and showed good behaviour with both his father and his mother who were separated. In the beginning it was a mystery where his formal personality for that age came from, until his concerns were defining the innate trait that made him behave in such a way. He felt distressed when he had to go to the blackboard, wondered why teachers would lower his grade because of this, something he was not perfect in not for lack of interest, but because of his own way of being. He was aware of the economic troubles at home and wanted to be an adult faster to become a good lawyer. He had good friends, he considered himself the "psychologist of the group" because everyone told him their problems, with a serious inconvenient, Marcos was making their problems his, with frequent concerns, his mind was unable to stop analyzing the disadvantages and possible alternatives of a situation. He even considered to stop studying because he thought it was a mistake to choose mathematics instead of a language or another subject. He didn't go out with friends or did activities for his age to review and re-review each exam. And he would feel distressed when at the end of an exam, some colleagues commented on what they answered, and he could spend several days with a pathological ruminative thinking. Everything was due to the over-stimulation caused by exams, the empathy toward the situation at home, the depth of processing all the stimuli and his sensory sensitivity.

3.3. Shyness and High Sensitivity

It is common that highly sensitive people identify themselves with phrases of the type "I've always been shy" or "my family and friends have always described me as too sensitive."

It seems incomprehensible, as they have had a similar upbringing as other people who do not need psychotherapy. This is due to the merging of both factors of high sensitivity and a difficult childhood, the result leading to perceive intensely, both pain and pleasure.

Jagiellowicz (2016) conducted experiments on brain activation, in which he found that HSP react more than others to photos of pets, cakes and nice things, also, they reacted more at pictures of spiders, snakes and unpleasant things, however the reaction to pleasant pictures was stronger in HSP with positive childhoods.

We could say that a highly sensitive person who has lived a difficult childhood, is more vulnerable to depression, anxiety, or shyness. This vulnerability is a consequence of having the trait and bad experiences.

It should be noted that no one is born shy, shyness is a

learnt fear, namely could be defined as fear of social judgement given by the lived experience and the assessment that the individual makes of the situation and the perceived sensation. Therefore, a bad experience may be responsible for generating what we call shyness.

Although it may seem that shyness is a trait of high sensitivity, it does not have to be. It is clear that shyness is a way to behave in certain social situations, which was acquired by bad experiences, meanwhile high sensitivity if it is an innate trait of temperament manifests itself as an awareness of the subtleties, as well as the tendency to feel overwhelmed by too many stimuli.

We understand as a stimulus a signal, both external and internal, which causes a reaction in the body. Therefore, an improved or advanced perception of the brain, which is not based on a quality of organs, but the brain itself capable of showing a deep information processing strategy and behaviour observed in highly sensitive people as a result of this quality are quite varied.

The consequences of feeling influenced by environment imperfections as well as the advantages and disadvantages of being born with high sensitivity, can be infinite, so life can take multiple paths and we can never know what would have happened if we would have taken a different path.

So far research has shown that 70% are introverts and 30% of highly sensitive people are extroverted. Eysenck (1953), describes introverted people as quiet individuals, withdrawn, reserved and distant. His work emphasizes more the physiological variables building a neurological theory of personality organized as a hierarchy.

Monjas and Caballo (2009) suggest that the term shyness refers to a set of heterogeneous phenomena existing lack of agreement on the definition of the construct, noting that alludes indiscriminately to terms such as shyness, social withdrawal, inhibition, introversion, isolation, lack of assertiveness and loneliness, arbitrarily, which has led to confuse these terms.

Shyness as a passive relationship style or inhibited, means not being able to express feelings, thoughts, and opinions, meaning these people allow others to not respect their feelings or opinions.

Regarding shyness as low sociability or low social acceptance, timidity, shyness, or passive style relationship, involve different terms between which there is some relationship.

Current theories explain the timidity by an interaction of variables, including temperament, attachment behaviour, peer relationships, stress, and context where the first experiences of social learning and attachment assume early interactions crucial to favor the predisposition to timidity. Failure in social situations will make the child believe that they are not able to face the challenge of relating, consolidating the conduct of shyness.

On its part, temperament, which is part of the innate character also influences when linked to the first social experiences and in highly sensitive children their innate trait coupled with the experience and temperament will determine the existence of social withdrawal.

Shyness as understood as a fear of social judgement, it is therefore an acquired behaviour like all fears. Despite this most parents believe that their child was born that way, shy or socially withdrawn, and resign themselves to this thinking it will improve with age which is why they do not usually seek therapy.

At school, teachers qualify these children as silent and fearful and since they do not present disruptive behaviours often even go unnoticed.

If we stop to think about our own past, who has not been shy at some point or in some situation in our life? In addition, all these children who we call timid, only show it in certain contexts, for example at home usually they are not, or in small intimate groups or at their best friend's house.

Highly sensitive children may seem shy because they

make a pause to observe before acting or leaving a social situation due to feeling overexcited at the time, or because they prefer to immerse in smaller groups trying discussions on deeper topics, philosophical or intimate.

Parents and teachers should be aware that for a HSC matching their temperament with the environment is everything, considering that as they grow, they will adapt to the world. But at younger ages it is recommended for optimal development of their personality to adapt their environment to their characteristics and thus avoid shyness.

The key is to keep a balance between stimulating them and protecting them from stimulation, although they are not to be deprived from making oral presentations in class, but finding the right time, giving them prior training time or establishing exhibitions gradually, i.e. from short ones in pairs or group to longer individual ones, and trying that every step is an achievement for the HSC so that feeling the success progressively and receiving positive reinforcement with praise will help avoid shyness or withdrawal in class activities.

Many children and adults have great psychological ability to avoid that the atmosphere generates them adversity or is conducive to risk in their development. We refer to risks such as mental, emotional, social or health problems.

This is how it was studied how it affects breeding patterns used by parents in the ability to develop such skill or psychological capacity. Investigations with highly sensitive children, show that they are able to develop the capacity to manage their negative emotions.

This is so because they get through the experience and social interaction, especially the HSC benefit from this ability, when growing up receive patterns of positive parenting. This indicates that HSC are more susceptible to the environment than other kids.

3.4. Self-criticism and High Sensitivity

Highly sensitive people are greatly affected by social injustices and are very self-critical, because of their desire for perfection, their analytical skills, and their great empathy. Injustice criticism and self-criticism can soon become pathological criticism, a term coined by psychologist Eugene Sagan to describe the negative inner voice that attacks and judges the individual. Although all people have an inner critical voice, some subjects maintain a permanent inner devastating voice which generates a continuous feeling of discomfort and inferiority consuming their self-esteem.

The negative internal dialogue makes the person

sensitive to their mistakes and their successes tend to go unnoticed which reinforces their negative self-perception. They continually remember their failures, although sometimes unconsciously, it's like having the mind set to think negative.

Pathological criticism is installed in the thought generating constant comparisons with others, seeing themselves at a disadvantage when performing such comparisons. HSP tend to set levels to reach perfection that are impossible be to be achieved, just hurting their self-concept.

All these situations are processed as failures or errors and turn increasingly into a broader list, therefore it would be ideal to treat these erroneous thought patterns on time, to prevent self-esteem from continuing to decline.

This way the brain of the individual stores in the memory words and negative images from their childhood, such as fat, clumsy, useless, etc., making it easier to remember the pejorative in situations of stress or discouragement.

This is another important reason to promote good parenting of the highly sensitive child since everything they have heard in childhood can influence their adulthood, considering also that they remember things that generate intense emotion.

A child that is not emotionally affected when a teacher calls them "awkward" in front of the classmates, will not have a problem later, but probably will not give it importance and forget it, but, in an HSC disparaging remarks from parents, relatives or teachers, cause marks since they feel it intensely and they will be more likely to remember it in the future.

We can say that pathological criticism is kept as a record in the individual failures, but not the achievements, where negative thoughts get linked, creating a feeling of low self-worth, encouraging memories of failures and mistakes and a tendency to exaggerate the flaws, causing a distorted self-image, and causing negative affect, discomfort, or guilt.

Self-criticism generates a momentary relief in the individual, giving rise to reoccurrences and unconsciously encourages the person's self critical and punishing behaviour even more.

To avoid this, the possible failures need to be analyzed and learn from experience, likewise, self-criticism causes a stress reaction to feared situations, i.e., those situations where the expectation is failure, favouring avoidance of the situation or lousy results.

Therefore, pathological, or negative criticism, that inner voice that generates discomfort in the individual, is something acquired and dependent on lived experiences. However, not all bad experiences can be avoided or control everything that other people say.

The best thing that you can do to help them is prepare them mentally to learn to interpret what they hear and give it proper value, considering their own knowledge of themselves, their traits and personality characteristics.

If you are a highly sensitive adult and you realize that your discomfort is due to this constant self-criticism filled with negative memories about yourself and generating a behaviour that puts the rights of others above your own, it's time to work the emotions and get a positive inner voice.

» Gabriela 7-year-old student

Gabriela's parents wondered if they were doing it well. It is quite common that parents question their own educational parenting styles. They said that their daughter was taking too long to have her breakfast on the days she had to go to school, had trouble to do her homework and had continued bickering between her and her little sister, among other things. Through relevant tests they ruled out possible shortfalls related to development. Both her father and mother had education related professions.

In addition, the private school which she was attending had good values. She expressed no complaints about classmates, nor there was any trace of conflict in the classroom. What was happening since everything seemed a fairy tale? They were not attending emotionally what the nature of their HSC wanted. Gabriela, a highly sensitive girl, and daughter of parents whose personalities were quite far from being highly sensitive people. It was necessary to change some element of communication. Gabriela's parents were doing it well since they had sufficient knowledge to establish an appropriate educational style. They just needed to know that they had to introduce transversely a change in the way they communicated the rules to their daughter. A 7-year-old girl who has highly sensitivity and understands the rules may need the message conveyed differently. As simple as changing an element in the communication process. Of course, they were doing it well since they did it with love and wisdom. It was not a matter of blame, rather, it was looking for solutions.

3.5. Social relations and High Sensitivity

In any social sphere, whether is family, friends, or the workplace, we can find people who cause discomfort to others, managing to diminish the emotional balance of the other. These are people who attack with insults, intended to generate feelings of guilt and when they find the occasion to humiliate, they take advantage of it.

They have a special ability to make the other person believe they are full of defects, not worthy of any privilege and even lower their self-esteem to the point of causing the other person severe anxiety and depression.

We could say that they are skilled in attacking sensitivity and that in turn they do it because of their own lack of self-esteem, fears and insecurities and often have a personality disorder.

Some highly sensitive people may become more vulnerable to manipulation by those who show a personality disorder, due to two traits, empathy, and sensitivity to stimuli. These characteristics make the highly sensitive person to easily "put on the skin" of the deranged individual and establish intense and close affective bonds at the beginning of the relationship, or until they realize the suffering that this person is causing them.

Each personality disorder has its own set of criteria or symptoms that professionals use to classify people into a clinical category and living together or regularly interacting with these types of people can be a source of great distress.

To which it should be added that most people with a personality disorder do not usually go to health professionals, because they do not recognize that what they think and feel may be a symptom of a disorder, and those who go is because there is another mental disorder in the background or because they have had a partner crisis, or because their conduct ends in a crime.

While we commented on the level of introversion of highly sensitive people, their shyness and possibility to "hook up" with people with problems, this will not lead such people to lead an isolated social life.

Sohst (2017), tells us about personal stories of women and men with high sensitivity, where he describes as exciting to have publicly recognized being a highly sensitive person and was surprised by the numerous positive comments he had received through social media.

The author considers that it is the senses that connect people to the environment despite those annoying noises unbearable to highly sensitive people, such as traffic noise or clock ticking. The perception of temperature or pain, which does not pose any problem to anyone, but detracts the well-being of an HSP. With regard to odours, a HSP can easily notice the smell of exhaust pipes from cars, or the smell of perfume after greeting a friend.

In general, and in line with the instructions of other authors regarding the environment of HSP, it could be said that HSP prefer to avoid those places where noise or smell makes it unpleasant.

So, if they have the opportunity to choose a house away from roads, shops, or, stay away from the crowd, and in search of tranquility, they usually go much further in the way they act, for example, by selecting well the restaurant to eat next Sunday, if the table is in a quiet and secluded place much better, and they also do not eat just anything to just spend the day, but select the menu well.

Although not only the senses of sight, hearing, smell, taste, or touch, mean finding harmony with the environment when we talk about an HSP, in terms of their personal relationships these have to be deep, they also seek a job in which to feel realized and that does not involve a long day, those that do not get a job with those characteristics, may become very stressed or develop psychosomatic diseases.

Regarding their relationship with others, they miss the loved ones that are far, and although they don't always make a good first impression in new situations, they end up being well valued by their friends and acquaintances.

References

Cattell, R.B. (1973). Personality and mood by questionnaire. Jossey-Bass Publishers.

Cattell, R.B. and Meredith, G.M. (1976). Psychological Theories of personality. Paidós Publishing House.

Digman, J.M. (1990). Personality structure: emergence of the five-factor model. Annual Review of Psychology, 50, 417–440. https://doi.org/10.1146/annurev.ps.41.020190.002221

Eysenck, H. J., and Eysenck, S. G.B. (1965). The Eysenck personality inventory. British Journal of Educational Studies, 14, 140–140. https://doi.org/10.2307/3119050

Jagiellowicz, J., Aron, A., Aron, E.N. (2016). Relation between the temperament trait of sensory processing sensitivity and emotional reactivity. Social Behavior and Personality, 44 (2), 185-200.

Monjas Casares. M. I. (2004) Is my son shy? Editorial Pyramid.

Monjas, I., and Caballo, V. E. (2002). Psychopathology and treatment of shyness in childhood in Caballo and Simon (Eds.), Manual of Clinical Psychology of Children and Adolescents (pp. 271-296). Editorial Pyramid.

Pluess, M., Belsky, J. (2015). Vantage sensitivity: genetic susceptibility to effects of positive experiences. M. Pluess (Ed.), Genetics of Psychological Well-Being, pp. 193-210. Oxford University Press.

Pluess, M., Assary, E., Lionetti, F., Lester, K. J., Krapohl, E., Aron, E., and Aron, A. (2018). Environmental Sensitivity in Children: Development of the Highly Sensitive Child Scale and Identification of Sensitivity Groups. Developmental Psychology. https://doi.org/10.1037/dev0000406

Sohst, K. (2017). The power of sensitivity. How to identify highly sensitive people and what we can learn from them. Editorial Ariel.

Suomi, S. J. (1991). Up tight and laid-back monkeys: Individual differences in the response to social challenges in S. Brauth, W. Hall and R. Dooling (Eds.), Plasticity of development. The MIT Press.

Suomi, S.J. (1997). Early determinants of behavior: evidence from primate studies. British Medical Bulletin, 53(1),170–184. https://doi.org/10.1093/oxfordjournals.bmb.a011598

Conclusions

The text addressed the highlights of the characteristics of highly sensitive people with particular attention to how they feel and how they live with their experiences and with others, and also addressed the most common defining personality characteristics knowing that they are mostly introverted, shy, and struggling to start social relationships.

They are often wise or covert leaders, altruistic, provide help if they are asked, know how to listen to others and care about them even before anyone can tell them the problem and for example, they need a timeout without the phone and refuse numerous or successive social events.

In short, if you are a highly sensitive person you need to know yourself, discover what you need and create the right environment for your own well-being. In children the optimal parenting, that is, a childhood surrounded by parents and teachers involved in the care of emotions, can become decisive to learn to live with the HSP trait.

www.ingramcontent.com/pod-product-compliance
Ingram Content Group UK Ltd.
Pitfield, Milton Keynes, MK11 3LW, UK
UKHW021924190726
13853UKWH00002B/839

9 788835 427766